HIKARI

LIGHTS AND SHADOWS

SHAYKH FADHLALLA HAERI

Much of human suffering and misery is due to mistaken identity.

HIKARI

LIGHTS AND SHADOWS

Zahra Publications

Published by Zahra Publications
www.shaykhfadhlallahaeri.com
info@shaykhfadhlallahaeri.com
www.zahrapublications.pub

Designed and typeset in South Africa by Quintessence Publishing

Set in 11 points on 13points, Garamond
Printed and bound by Lightning Source

ISBN (Printed Version) — Paperback: 978-1-7764901-0-3

Table Of Contents

Introduction

"Hikari" is a Japanese word that translates to "light" in English. It can refer to literal light, like sunlight or illumination, and metaphorical light, symbolising hope, clarity, enlightenment, or positivity. The word "Hikari" is often used in various contexts in Japanese culture, including literature, art, and everyday language, to convey different shades of meaning related to light and its symbolic significance.

Reality emanates from the perpetual cosmic Oneness that radiates numerous patterns of lights which brings about life. As evolved human beings, any link that connects us to the origin, gives us comfort, ease and joy. We are privileged to have numerous links to this Oneness. Language can help us to connect and unify, so does a beautiful scene, so do all our major senses—through attraction and repulsion. The following short bursts of insights are steps towards being at one with the light within the heart.

All our ambitions and drives ultimately lead us to the origin and creation of cosmic Oneness. Truth is one. Reality is one. Boundless eternal life is one, emanating from the One.

Shaykh Fadhlalla Haeri

2024

Reality & Truth

Our life is balanced between the infinate and eternal and the limitations of space and time and our conditioned consciousness. This earthly conciousness emanates from the boundless conciousness or the quantum field of Reality that is beyond the mind to comprehend. Whatever exists has been touched by the power of reality and truth, even though it may be fleeting. The mystery of life is due to the fact that boundless and eternal truth envelops everything known and unknown. It is not a puzzle that can ever be resolved. It can only be known by transcending from our conditioned conciousness and its limitation to this higher zone from where everything emanates.

Spring blooms, radiating life.
Local and universal effulgence of grace.
Visible and hidden.
Two zones from One.

When the voice of Truth
reached the desert of my heart,
it bloomed and perfumed
paradise on earth.

When the sage spoke,
words of separation and distance were erased.
The original Light
confirmed destiny.

Without drama or fuss,

Please be honest.

Facts and earthly realities

are the earthly manifestations

of the permanent Real.

Be Real,

please.

Truth is ever-present

ever-constant,

never touched

by uncertainty or doubt.

Eternally perfect.

Small and short-lived

hell or paradise

on earth.

Prelude to perpetual states

after death.

You feel crammed and that is real.

You feel trapped and that too is real.

They say, “be patient” or “stop time”.

That also is true.

You seek eternal perfection,

sung by your soul.

Even though you have doubt and suspicion,

you wish to trust and believe

the cosmic wali

containing all.

Truth is ever perfect.
Its light reveals perfection at every moment
even when it is judged otherwise.
How could it be otherwise?
Could there be anything other than
perfection in diluted versions?

Silence says it all;
absence has it all;
darkness hides it all
within mindlessness.
Where death veils life,
reason reveals a spark of truth.

The truth is all-encompassing,
its light within us all.
When the illusion of two-ness is reduced
the evidence of effulgent Oneness,
overwhelms all.

Gift of Life & Death

Our human consciousness is balanced between attraction and repulsion, darkness and light, knowledge and ignorance, alive or dead. Life is a great mystery from the Ever-Living and whatever it touches makes it obsessed with it. Therefore, the fear of death is natural. Transcending that fear is a higher nature. Life is eternal in its nature.

Life is an eternal and boundless divine force
that appears to be conditioned
by each person or living entity
to observe and interact with ever-changing
shadows through the ego-self.
The soul transmits the energy
that illumines these shadows.

Ease always comes with its twin:
difficulty.
All earthly experiences are
temporarily balanced dualities,
energised by the constant soul.

To experience lasting joy,
you need to be stripped of all mental conditions
regarding space, time and identity
and be in a state of neutral presence and
cheerfulness.
The ego-self is now a faint shadow in the effulgent
light of the soul.

Good judgment is vital for quality life
but is relative and confined to a specific event and
time.
It is helpful in calibrating with the perfect soul
within and in reducing the darkness of the lower
self.

Life—a cosmic treasure conditioned by our senses,
preparing us for its eternal and boundless nature,
when the barriers of body and mind are removed.
That is the purpose of life on earth.

If you can't live in total harmony and joy
with yourself,
how can you ever expect to be tranquil and happy
with anyone else?
Everyone has the same challenge,
to transcend the lower self.

Love is the ultimate bond that unifies,
and like life, its field of energy is everywhere.
You can only experience it
if you leave other mental and emotional states
and simply embrace One.

You are not really ill nor well.
As a caterpillar-self, morphing to a butterfly.
Spirit life on earthly transit,
work in progress
towards Home.

To hear more, close your eyes.

To see more, close your ears.

To know more, lose your mind.

Steps to real beingness,

Where all signals and receptors are at One.

The recluse sage in the mountain pass,
Providing shleter and food for whomever was passing,
was asked why his smile danced.
"To welcome life and the presence of the sacred,
that is our purpose."

"What is my end?" he asked.

"A vibration returned,

as your beginning

emerging from eternity,

without identity,

so is your end.

Then you had emerged then submerged."

Whatever experiences life
will experience death,
with fear and disdain,
except for the eternal soul
released by death
from earthly traps.

Earthly life may be short.
But if you can stop time,
or step out of time then,
boundless eternity
shines most clearly from beyond death.

After death,
eternal time becomes clear.
With delights of loss,
whatever was far or near,
in harmony and delight with higher consciousness,
with temporary traces of a past.

The joy of losing oneself
beyond thoughts and identity.
Like falling in love
or becoming one with Cosmic Oneness
through the gift of death.

The desire to celebrate a special occasion is the natural drive to the perpetual timeless. The divine soul showing its presence like a flame. Then gone from our sights a human limitation revealing divine manifestation.

Human Consciousness, Ego & Illusion

Life can be experienced through the gift of consciousness, which can only be appreciated when it relates to a certain unveiling of what was unknown. A healthly baby begins to connect with different experiences until it becomes familiar with the changing environment around it. In a few years time, the child behaves in a manner that connects it with the outer environment, interactively. Soon, the personality that is concerned with preserving life and experiencing its manifestations in an agreeable way. Within a few more years, a sense of ego is developed. With it, rises the illusion of what is good or not. The pure life force has to be filtered through ever-changing values and illusions so that our interactions widen and deepen.

Without reflection, permission, or authorisation,
we created a noisy world
with much suffering and confusion.
From birth to death–a universal blip.
Experienced with increasing anxiety, why?

We have two duties.
One to our earthly consciousness
and ever-changing situations
and the other to our heavenly soul and spirit.
It radiates constant Life.

All actions come with confusion and stress.
Regretting departure from stillness,
where the eternal light of pure consciousness
resides.

Are you serious in calling your experience real?

What about deep sleep?

Where are you after death?

What are you?

Who are you?

All shades of the Real.

The impact of any loss is greater than that of gain.

Life on earth is to discover

the eternal soul within you,

all you have is time,

and its loss is the real tragedy.

We are gripped by fear–all of us.
Almost paralysed–all of us.
We may wake up one day
by grace of hope and fear.
To celebrate Life's perfect way.

Material wealth and security may enhance
aspects of humanity,
but can also be detrimental
to the rise of spiritual intelligence awakening to
the divine soul.

Your soul never ages,
the body and mind do.
Aging may enable us to realise
the eternal soul,
connecting origin and destiny.

A clear mind is a great gift of nature.

A pure heart illumines one's path and is a divine grace.

Most of us are muddled in between.

Every human drive is towards the perfect soul.
Whatever is alive quests for higher attributes
radiadated from the soul.
Come on now and return Home.

Generosity is a divine attribute

radiating from the soul

and meanness is its dark shadow

relating to the ego self.

All that is regarding as virtues or vices follow a

similar pattern.

Whilst acting with proper attention and skillful application,
a flexible attitude to failure is necessary for a healthy inner state,
more than the actual outcome of the project.
Success is balanced by failure in life and the enlightened attitude brings about a wholesome understanding of balance.

Trust and faith enhance human quality.
We are naturally driven to trust and believe
in what is tangible or intangible.
This is the soil that produces hope and
interactions in our world.

A baby trusts the mother
without knowing what trust is.
Eventually, belief and trust may lead
to complete trust in the moment
and its perfection.

I know you well,
as well as I know me.
Mean and generous,
easy and difficult,
and everything in between
–ever reliable in your unrealiability.

Not easy to save anyone from suffering.
There are numerous scapegoats around,
Humans and other creatures, close or far.
Even rogue politicians are a credible target.
Everything is there to prolong the veils of
ignorance and illusion.

Obsession with appearance

to look beautiful and well groomed.

reflect the soul's perfection

but can lead to inflated ego.

No one to talk to.

They cannot hear,

ears blocked.

Nodding heads, dim comprehension, locked in

dark illusion.

Personal deceptions and global confusion.

Everyone anxious.

Love and harmony in distortion.

Time to embrace silence and absence.

The ego-self, safe at home with its illusions and props,
demanding freedom and happiness
at all times,
promoted as purpose of life.

The ego-self causes confusion
and as for the suffering soul,
it radiates goodnes and light
eternally.

Everyone yearns for the freedom to choose.
The best of all is
free of regrets or sorrow
declared by the soul,
modified by the ego.

A confused mind is a curse.

It leads to chaos and breakdowns.

To increase this confusion with alcohol or drugs

is the ultimate ignorance and destruction.

The ignorant remain self-concerned
with survival and benefits.
While the intelligent seek what is beyond
limitations of time and space,
the eternal and boundless.

Your soul is connected

to the Source of all knowledge.

Its shadow self also yearns for that state.

I asked, 'Who are you?'
and you explained what you do.
Not easy to answer,
except for those dead or the rare few
who have gone past
the illusion of the self.

Loss usually brings sadness
except for the ego-self.
A great triumph,
that leads to supreme gladness.

Desires, Hopes & Fears

To interact with life around us, we are propelled by the forces of desires, needs, hopes and fears. We naturally look for fulfilment in life and avoidance of pitfalls, regrets, sorrows and guilt. Our path in life takes us towards higher consciousness with least distractions and fallbacks.

I want better;

I want bigger;

I want more to no end.

I want the eternal

without end,

and I want even more.

Grace is boundless and my ego is between fear

and sorrow.

No end to needs
increasing stress and anxiety,
and other dark shadows.
Then the moon whispered,
'Half is darkness and
the other half bright.'

What do you want?
Not important, you say.
You are a fool caught in the chains of desires.
Only God can help you,
but you don't know how to reach Him.
As He is closer than closeness,
no distance nor absence.

Your story, my story,
each story declares purpose and quest.
Where is the end to hopes and desires?
Where is the beginning?
Where are we?
More urgently,
who are we?

Always looking for a purpose –
useful and beneficial.
Always groping in darkness, confused.
Propelled by fear and hope, always.
One day you may hear the angel ask,
where is the end?
Now you are fortunate,
realising that any beginning or end
are inseperable.

Supreme cosmic gift of life,
seen and unseen,
on earth and heavens.
Eternally present,
Radiating
from sacred presence.

The sage said.

'It is all a test,

and no one asked

who is testing who.

Whereas truth is One.'

Then he lauged and said.

'Truth is eternally Real!'

I was asked to tell the story.
A real story must be sad, so be prepared.
The illusory self always seeks to be glad.
The light of the Real will put an end to all illusions.
All our fantasies and darknesses that hint at the
other side of life's brightness.

You say you don't like that.
But now you change your mind.
How is that possible?
How can change be constant?
No wonder we are confused.
We invent a purpose,
to reduce the darkness
by distractions.

Self-interest motivates everyone.
But the self is in
constant change,
negating durable happiness.
But find me those
not propolled
by absurd ambitions!

Our earth moves
with some predictability
and much uncertainty.
Such is life.
When the outcome of work becomes predictable,
we are bored and uninterested.
Naturally a safe cove
perched on vast oceans
with the illusion of stability.

Our natural drive to believe and trust,
is often accompanied by frustrations,
disappointments and blaming others.
Accept personal ignorance
and false trust
in the elusive self.

Naturally conflicted
between doubt and trust,
without faith and
hope is lost
and faith not attaining trust
is an illusion
leading to a universe
of doubts and darknesses.

Fear and sorrow often accompany
pain and pleasure,
all within time and space.
Whereas bliss and joy relate to the heart and soul
not limited to basic consciousness
and can be pure and durable.

Memory is a great gift,

whereas loss of memory

may be less disturbing of natural peace.

Fear of loneliness is a powerful drive
that can lead to despair and misery
or lead to the reality of
existence and life–eternal cosmic Oneness.

Our desire for perfection and beauty
is fraught with the dangers
of deception, concealments and cover ups
of faults, failures and ugliness.

Fear and hope permeate all life experiences.

We fear the confusion of dispersion and differences,

and hope for connecteness and unity.

We often think that
others may like what we like.
Any similarity or agreement is like a bridge
towards Oneness.

Religious faith, belief and practice can bestow
some modesty, humility and patience,
but can also produce arrogance, vanity
and smug behaviour.

There is enough space for all that exists
and there is enough time for everything
to reach its potential always.
Divine Generosity is ever-present.
Everywhere and always.

Knowledge, Governance & Leadership

With maturity and intelligence, every being tries to maintain a wholesome integrity as well as to maintain life within themselves. Self-preservation and striving for goodness and benefit are natural drives in us towards higher consciousness. Every living entity is charged with responsible governance of their body and mind. Wherever there are individuals, there will also be the collective, that is where the desire for good leadership arises. An individual who acted and behaved well for themselves may qualify for collective leadership, otherwise, it can cause serious collective suffering.

You don't know,
and perhaps,
will never know–
but welcome to life and the drive
to know.
The drive to hope,
the drive to better destiny,
and the life within–
eternal Truth.

They don't know me, nor do I.
Yet, I admire me. Mostly there is only I.
Mostly in secret,
revealed through inner eyes.
One day we may meet,
when no day remains,
and the original light shines bright.

Life after death is often
the main gateway for humans
to the cosmic courtyard
of eternal unity.

All along, I deceived myself
with illusions of comfort of ignorance and
darkness,
and now I am doing it again,
with wisdom and knowledge,
but less content.

It is natural to look up to
someone who knows and helps
in our quest to connect
and leave the darkness
of ignorance, to be closer to
the soul's cosmic connection.

Normal intelligence leads

to better choices and actions.

Super intelligence leads to no choice

and the end of identifying yourself

with the actor

playing a role.

He taught me what to do,
more so what not to do.
Knowledge saved me from darkness.
ignorance saved me from blinding light.
Humanity showed me humility
and beauty in all things,
especially you and me,
and all that is alive.

It is not unusual to find a
a religious teacher not living the teaching,
and that is why
many people doubt the efficacy of religion or
God.

It is natural to follow and expect.
Also natural
to be often disappointed,
as there was another with greater skill.
Then your insight may reveal a unique reality,
One and only One
above the top,
ever Supreme.

It is a natural to look
for a leader more excellent than others–
Super excellence emanates from the soul in the
heart.
Wisdom and kindness precede from good
humanity.

After many battles and years of bloodshed,

the kingdom was lost.

New power emerged only to disappear

more gruesomely again than the past.

Then more accidents, mistakes and ignorance.

That is how history is invented.

Most natural events occur in cycles.
Often with slight variations until they end.
Truth is neither new nor old,
it is ever alive.
Because of that constancy,
we experience variations in time.

They mourned the controversial statesman with
carefully selected events,
he was conflicted but put up a confident facade.
He did it for the sake of the others, he said.
A courageous reporter pointed the absurdities
but was rebuked.
Honesty is dangerous.

To be followed and obeyed
successfully,
you need to have followed someone
successfully.
But there is no guarantee.

Perfections & Destiny

Perfection has been limited to human desires and expectations, whereas, all that occurs is due to seen and unseen forces. Human life on earth is to practice the highest level of awareness so that we flow along nature towards the end of a chapter or event, which we call destiny.

Desire for reliability, stability,
contentment and bliss
are beams of conciousness
emanating from the soul.
A mysterious divine power
residing in the heart
and source of life.

Without an appropriate reference or perspective,
any plan or action may be regretted or
considered incomplete
in a different time or place.

Due to enlightenment
you witness perfection
in every situation.
To be in that state,
accept personal judgement,
then drop it.
Then look at the perfect links
of cause and effect that lead to the event,
all follows perfection.

Perfection is the nature of reality,

every moment,

not coinciding with our expectations

or local judgment,

witness the Ever-Perfect,

now and always.

All is falling apart,
loss of sincerity, loyalty, and most of all,
honesty.
Thus the universal rise
of false personal identity and ego-self.

Always dependant.

Links of past, present, and future thoughts.

Accepting and rejecting,

desperately insecure,

uncertain,

praying for the constant.

Is it all due to the mind or
in spite of it?
All appears as real and yet
I know it is not.
So, what is the fuss about?
To discover meanings and new forms?
What was there before you and I
is here now.

Thoughtful and polite,
each member of
the meditating group
earnestly hoping one day to know themselves.
One drug addict smiled hesitantly and said,
'My only desire is to lose myself,
I think that there is no self.'

You love to celebrate.
You love the big party without end.
No one knows anyone,
but pretend otherwise.
We long for escapes and distractions,
whilst perfect destiny is ever there,
awaiting attention
and eternal embrace.

Time, Presence & Boundlessness

Human life on Earth is experienced within conditioned consciousness which allows constant change and the advent of new situations due to the illusion of the flow of time, within space. Our consciousness functions within space and time but its origin is from beyond these limitations. With practice and grace, we can experience the timelessness of pure presence. When you are occupied with difficulties and insecurities, time seems to move slowly. If you can focus on the moment itself, you may be touched by an exhilarating experience of no time and no space. Through chanting, self-hypnosis or other means, you may experience that infinite moment more easily.

A glimpse of
the real you
flashed upon its shadow,
leaving its trace
from eternal timelessness –
the sacred Origin.

Our experience of time
varies in speed.
It moves slowly
when we are bored or unhappy
and passes rapidly
when we are absorbed or connected.

The experience of time is the link to
the eternal and timeless.
Our conciousness of passing time
encourages transcendence
to where there is no time and no boundaries–
the soul within.

Time is a miracle perfect, ever there and eternal
and yet races along fast.
Within time you experience
boredom or delight,
or for a time, being trapped or free,
all changes from the Constant.

Time is considered most valuable,
until you experience timelessness–
an eternal nature gifted by life, for all times and places.
The cosmic Divine touch
of boundless generosity.

With the dark ego-self
time moves slowly
with the light of your soul
you may even lose the notion of time.

Time is like a sacred rope.

It can tie you down

and suffucate you

or be a heavenly rope

to climb back to eternity.

Peace and silence,
womb of all creations.
Producing dual challenges
of desires, fears, hopes, dreams and illusions
of what is real.
All awaiting rediscovery
of the cosmic mother.

Mighty power of presence
Enabling shadows to
appear and then vanish.
All within time and space.
Only presence remains forever.

It passed so fast.

Distance and time vanished.

Then came back,

ever so slowly,

with total disregard

for all

movement and change.

Ever present,

Divine,

Eternal.

On his death bed, the sage was begged
for ultimate wisdom.
Softly, he said, 'Be in the moment.
Always present.
Life is forever
and you are a temporary agent.'

Every movement emerges from stillness,
expressing an aspect of the vastness
dormant within silence.
Miracle of treasures.

Infinite Light & Illuminated Conclusions

Whatever exists has emanated from the mysterious divine Light and Power. We experience our day-to-day life through lights and shadows. The origin of all that is known and unknown, is Divine mystery which appeared first as life itself and from thereon, everything else that exists. Our life on earth is to prepare us for a higher zone of consciousness where body, mind and other illusions and filters, are no longer there. Before you were born, there was only the perfect cosmic Light, and the same will be experienced after death.

Curiosity starts with what is near and relevant
then broadens in space and time.
Instant contentment is in the instant,
where ease and peace prevails
and the light of your soul
conceals fears and darknesses,
as reflected from the ego-self.

Humans experience memory and identity
as a shade or veil the light of Reality.
With the rise of consciousness of the shadow self,
the experience of separation and differences
cause fears, sorrow and other distractions
which are dealt with by reason and rationality.

When you feel weighed down,
Remember that everything has a time limit
except life.
It is limitless.
Patience can lead
to the shore of timelessness.

Shadows and confusion
appear as the ego-self,
the other side of inner light,
sacred soul ever-constant,
providing life.

Your inner light
revealing,
strands of shadows,
honored guests in flight.
Propelled by
Eternal Presence.
The mighty gift
of divine Light
and its cosmic well.

Give me the real news after which,
there is no more news,
good or bad.
Then I am content
with eternal time.

Everyone is the same
with fears and hopes,
differences are
in clarity, direction and drive
towards awakening,
to the ever-present Light.

When I discovered

I am not an ever-elusive self

and this shadow is illumined by the eternal soul.

The quest of self discovery ended.

Treat others as you wish for yourself –

a wise counsel.

One day you may go past dualities.

One day the light of Truth may dazzle you.

That is the trick of absolute Oneness.

Why should I do good?
Why love and generosity for all?
Why sacrifice for others?
Oneness reveals that there is no other,
Only the One.
Then you say it is precisely why we should act
with no self-concern.
What about concern for others?

Your soul knows it all.
It is constant, perfect, and self-contained.
Its shadow self is ever-changing.
Labelled as ego,
veiling the heavenly soul,
on a short earthly journey,
returning home.

"Where is hell and paradise?"

The voice of Truth answered,

"In the infinite unseen,

appearing diluted on earthly mirrors,

to assure us of where we are at

and where we are heading towards."

The joy of the rose perfume,

owes much to

what has nourished the plant,

don't ask what!

All emerges from the One,
appears in every shape and form;
attraction and repulsion governs all.
Love is the pluralities powerful connector
between entities.

Death,

the natural end to the story

of birth

and entry back to higher consciousness.

Boundless and eternal.

In reality, there is only Truth,

The Reality.

Timeless–and present everywhere, always.

www.ingramcontent.com/pod-product-compliance
Lightning Source LLC
Chambersburg PA
CBHW051652040426
42446CB00009B/1106
* 9 7 8 1 7 7 6 4 9 0 1 0 3 *